LYNN PISTACCHIO

Empathic Listening

Becoming the Person Everyone Loves to Talk To

Contents

1

Chapter 1

Introduction:

"**M**ost people do not listen with the intent to understand; they listen with the intent to reply." –Stephen Covey

We are born with the gift of hearing. We hear our parents speaking while we are still a fetus in the womb. We hear noises and different sounds. Oftentimes after being born, a young infant is accustomed to these sounds, being unafraid and sometimes comforted when they hear them. Examples of this phenomenon are music, laughter, blow dryers and vacuums.

We come to learn what these noises mean as we hear them growing up.

So what is the difference between hearing and listening?

Hearing is recognizing there is a sound. It's the process of perceiving that sound. Listening is an interpretation of what that sound means. Listening is the learned process of identifying and understanding what the sound is and what it means.

As we grow in years, we often forget that we need to refine the language of listening to sounds. Some people can ignore a repetitive sound while remaining focused on something else. Others need some background noise while they work or go about their daily tasks.

This book is about conversation and communication skills. It's about how to be a person people love to talk to. Making good conversation takes 2 people. It requires a talking person and a listening person. Notice I did not say a hearing person... there is a difference! Knowing the difference will strengthen your relationships, not only personally, but in your chosen career field.

This book allows you to grow in confidence to handle the tough situations in life. Knowing the difference could easily allow you to reach those who are struggling. Knowing the difference between hearing and listening could change someone's life.

Why is it important to be a good listener? The bottom line to that question can be found in how you treat people. If you are a Peanuts Gang fan, you've heard the WAA WAA sounds played when their parents or teachers talk. All parents believe that our children hear us using the WAA WAA sound. What we say goes in one ear and out the other. No instructions are followed, and what we actually said can't be remembered or repeated. It makes parents irritated, angry and frustrated. Voices are raised. We've all been there.

For a moment, consider the next few questions. While listening to others, do you hear WAA WAA or are you hearing the actual words and processing them into thought? Do you routinely forget what a spouse or child has asked you to do? Do you have trouble focusing on verbal instructions at work? How about dreading conversations with family members? I have! Are your co-workers or customers easily frustrated while talking to you?

Could you benefit from learning to listen more empathic and actively?

What if you were a person others trusted more in conversation? Would you like to feel that people trust your judgment or opinions more? Have you ever considered that the conversations you have with others can affect their self-esteem, making them feel valued or even under-valued?

I am glad that you answered yes to some of those questions. That means you value people and they value you.

Investing in yourself and in other people always makes a differ-ence. Let's get started!

"Good conversations with the right people are priceless." — Anonymous

2

Chapter 2

The Art of Active Listening

"Being heard is so close to being loved that for the average person, they are almost indistinguishable." —David W. Augsburger

What is active listening?

Active listening is a way of listening and responding to another person that will improve your mutual understanding.

What is Empathic listening?

Empathic listening means being aware of, and understanding, the speaker's feelings and emotions, as well as the words that they are using. This means consciously trying to understand the meaning of what they are saying—but also what is behind the words, and what they are not saying.

What really is active listening and what role does it play in emphatic communication?

Active listening is a mental skill that anyone can develop. If you learn to focus on the people you are talking to and ignore the surrounding distractions in their area, you are using a component of active learning. It is an intentional technique and process with long-term results. To apply this skill, you have to be aware of a few details as your time together talking starts and continues. Are you experiencing a language barrier? Do you understand the slang or design of the other person's speech? Are the details of what the other person is saying making sense in the context of the topic? Is it a subject you are interested in? How many details are involved? There are several factors involved just in the speech part of the conversation?

Perhaps you are in a crowded restaurant. Is it a loud environment? Do you or the other person hear well? Do you need to speak loudly to talk? Is the conversation difficult? All of these items can hinder active listening. Active listening is giving your undivided attention to many small, yet important details AND to the person who is doing the talking.

Most importantly, active listening makes the person feel influential enough to listen to. It makes them feel what they have to say worth talking about. Your actions are also conveying that what they are saying is worth listening to.

Empathic listening is similar in that you notice many details, but you are more importantly seeing and sensing the *emotions and feelings* behind what you are watching.

You may be in a crowded, noisy restaurant. Is the noise making your guest feel irritable or anxious? Are they nervously speaking with their hands? Are the fidgety? Signs like this give you a clue that things are not alright, even if the other person is saying they are fine. The actions and the words do not match.

Empathetic communication helps people understand what others think, feel, and see.

Think of it as listening with your eyes to what is and is not being said out loud.

What is the science behind active listening?

According to one study conducted at the University of California, Berkeley, actively listening to someone activates various parts of the brain. When participants listened to a speaker describe a personal tale, their brain activity coordinated with the speaker.

Listening improves relationships by demonstrating awareness, concern, and respect. To listen well, you must put your agenda and need to be heard to the side. Listening needs to be done without an element of judgment. Being able to talk without interruption is a liberating, freeing experience for many people. It allows the speaker to feel accepted for their views. You don't need to agree with what their views are, but allowing them the safe space to vocalize their thoughts and feelings (without judgment) is very healing. It allows social behavior to improve because it is such a positive experience.

As the speaker becomes aware that you are listening and interested in what is being said, the reward center in their brain is activated. When this happens, you are regarded as an important and trusted ally. It is a key component in establishing a strong relationship between two people.

Are there benefits for the listener when they practice active empathic listening? Of course!

Whenever you actively engage in listening, your brain's neural pathways associated with attention and comprehension become stronger and more efficient. It enhances your cognitive abilities, memory retention, and problem-solving skills, which will help you achieve success in various areas of life.

"Validation is one of the most powerful tools we have in our toolkit for changing the world" –Marianne Williamson

3

Chapter 3

Decoding Nonverbal Cues

"The most important thing in communication is hearing what isn't said."
— **Peter Drucker**

We as humans communicate in two distinct ways: Verbal and Nonverbal.

Whether it's oral or written, verbal communication uses words to convey a message.

Nonverbal communication is the movements and actions displayed by our body, whether we are talking or not talking. We are always conveying some sort of communication unconsciously. An example of this is crossing your legs or arms while just sitting.

We are always sending signals.

According to experts, around 70% of all human interactions involve nonverbal communication, which means we only convey 30% of our messages through written or spoken communication.

Nonverbal communication, or "clues" sometimes answer for us without the use of words. We nod our head for a yes or no answer. We put our hand up for someone to hold on or hold up. Humans use many of these clues without consciously thinking. They are symbols and cues we have learned since birth, mainly because our language skills have not been developed. Our cues are a rich source of information about what is going on in our current situation emotionally. Are you having a frustrating day? Typical clues are the tone of your voice, the frown on your face, the furrow on your forehead and eyebrow region. Oftentimes we don't realize we are telling on ourselves.

Learning to decipher people's nonverbal information provides insight to others around you, allowing them time to decide how to proceed with their conversations according to your body language.

According to Positive Psychology, bodily communication cues include:

Facial expression

- Facial expression is possibly the most important nonverbal communication. We can share a message of anger, surprise, disappointment, fear, or sadness simply through facial expressions, such as raised eyebrows or the shape of the mouth.

Gaze

- How much time and when or if we look at a speaker conveys a level of interest. As we talk, it can also provide us with details of our listener's reactions to what we have said.

Eye contact

- Eye contact is more direct than gaze; it conveys a great deal, including anger, interest, and even attraction.

Gestures

- We can frame what we are saying or illustrate our points using physical movements. They may show emotion (using a pointed finger or a clenched fist) or add information to our words, illustrating a shape, size, or movement.

Posture

- When we physically turn toward someone as they speak or lean forward, we convey interest; facing away or leaning backward can suggest a lack of interest or even boredom. Posture, such as sitting with legs and arms crossed tightly, may express being anxious or uptight.

Physical closeness

- Our degree of comfort with physical closeness can vary depending on culture and connection with the other person. For example, the intimate zone (6–18 inches or 15–45 centimeters) may be reserved for close friends, relatives, or someone we have an established relationship with. The social zone (4–12 feet or 1.2–3.65 meters) includes those who are less well known, and the public zone (over 12 feet or 3.65 meters) is for public gatherings.

Clothes

- What you wear can communicate a great deal, including social and occupational standing, ethnicity, conformity, and gender identity. Different age and social groups may respond in various ways depending on the clothes we wear.

Grooming

- Important information is conveyed by how we care for ourselves, such as being clean and tidy, styling hair, and removing/not removing body hair.

Body language and nonverbal cues are worth learning and do become easier to notice the more you work at it. The more time you spend with people you know and understand, the quicker you'll be able to read each person individually. Parents with infants and toddlers are a great example. Having a child in your care teaches you the signs of that baby being hungry, tired, and even when they need a diaper change.

The key is to stop and be present when you are around people. Take a moment and focus on what is going on around you and the others in your area. Pay attention and take mental notes. See what the difference might be between the person's words and their actions with body language. Become aware of what they aren't saying in words that give you greater understanding of their true feelings and emotions. Given enough practice and willingness to notice behavior in those around you, you will become a proficient and effective communication in no time.

"The most important thing in communication is hearing what isn't said."
— **Peter Drucker**

4

Chapter 4

Improving Emotional Intelligence

"**E**motional intelligence allows us to respond instead of react." — Unknown

What is the definition of emotional intelligence (EI)?

The ability to monitor and control one's own emotions is referred to as emotional intelligence (EI), also known as emotional quotient (EQ).

A high EI reduces mental stress through instilling self-awareness, self-regulation, and effective communication skills. This will help you gain confidence and become emotionally stronger.

What Are the Signs of Emotional Intelligence?

Harvard Professional Development defines Emotional Intelligence as a set of skills and behaviors that can be learned and developed. Here are some telltale signs of people with low EQ and those with high EQ.

People with low EQ:

- Often feel misunderstood
- Get upset easily
- Become overwhelmed by emotions
- Have problems being assertive

People with high EQ:

- Understand the links between their emotions and how they behave
- Remain calm and composed during stressful situations
- Are able to influence others toward a common goal
- Handle difficult people with tact and diplomacy

To be a person with stronger Emotional Intelligence adaptability, there are four areas to focus on: self-awareness, self-regulation, social awareness, and social skills:

- **Self-awareness**: The ability to identify and understand your emotions and the impact we have on others is called self-awareness.
- **Self-regulation:** Self-awareness leads to self-regulation, which is the ability to manage these emotions and behaviors.

Once we know how we feel, we can start to control them and keep the emotions and impulses that are bothering us in check.

· **Social awareness:** Social awareness means being able to understand how others feel, and one way to do this is by showing empathy.

· **Social skills:** These skills, such as influence, conflict management, teamwork, and the ability to inspire others, help you build and keep healthy relationships in all parts of your life.

Strengthening your skills to improve your emotional life and compliment your active listening skills can be simple, it just takes practice, an open heart and an open mind when caring about people.

Practice the art of listening with your ears, your heart, and your eyes.

Learn and practice to actively empathize with the person you are talking to. It's not being sympathetic as many people expect it to be. Take yourself into their shoes and ask what you would do, feel or how you'd react if you were in the same situation.

It's applying the gift of wanting to understand their perspective that makes empathy so powerful.

Finally, reflect on the many people you have talked to over the course of time. How did they respond or react during a situation? Would they react the same today? If so, why not? What can you learn from that situation? What about yourself? How have you changed, or how could you improve?

No matter the answers you give to these questions, take the time to celebrate. You are taking steps by reading these thoughts, making plans on how to implement these ideas into your daily relationships, and moving forward into a new chapter of life.

You are on a journey many people don't care enough to take.

"Too often we underestimate the power of a touch, a smile, a kind word, a listening ear, an honest compliment, or the smallest act of caring, all of which have the potential to turn a life around." Leo Buscaglia

5

Chapter 5

The Pitfalls of Judgment and Ego

"If you judge people, you have no time to love them."
–Mother Teresa

"Ego trip: a journey to nowhere" –Robert Half

What is Judgement in relation to relating to people?

Judging means to form an opinion about someone or something based on thoughts, feelings, and evidence. This often occurs within the first few minutes of meeting someone. When you judge a person, you assess their character in order to determine if they are safe.

As a human, we learn to judge situations, places, and evidence to keep us from harm or danger. We can have good judgement and bad judgement depending on circumstances, upbringing and our past experiences.

When it comes to relationships, our judgement of people can have a negative effect. In today's society, people use it as a put-down and to single others out as "different" or unacceptable. When this happens, Judgement becomes character assassination. It's a hurtful and demeaning experience and emotionally damaging to the recipient.

Time and time again, judging is frequently based on superficial information or partial facts when you criticize others. You will be less likely to believe your automatic assumptions if you are curious about the person instead of being critical.

The act of curiosity enables one to inquire and acquire knowledge before arriving at a conclusion. Talking to someone and learning who they are can help you gain more insight into their choices. Your view on their newly shared information tends to be more positive and less automatic when you get to know someone.

Knowing what others are going through as well as their past experiences helps you learn to understand their journey with more compassion and understanding.

Do we have to actually judge someone? No, just learn about them because you are interested and want to "see" situations and ideas through their eyes.

What is ego?

By definition, an ego is a persons' belief in themselves and how important they are. It helps define their level of pride and self-worth in themselves. It helps them decide their importance in the world around them.

We all develop an ego, whether big or small. When used correctly, the ego can help you build confidence in yourself. Learning to control your ego will benefit and transform your relationships personally and professionally.

The way we show or use our ego impacts our capacity to effectively communicate with people and comprehend their own personal egotism or feelings.

What if you could interact with others without getting your ego involved? I believe we can if we choose to look at ourselves and identify what our motives are in this conversation.

Once we have a more in-depth understanding of ourselves, we will better understand how to listen and interact. This helps us talk in a way that's friendly, secure, and interesting instead of comparing or judging the other person.

Judgement is the core of a wounded ego.

Combining your judgment and ego together in personal and professional settings can be a recipe for disaster. When we judge, the ego becomes smug. Our egos love it when we feel powerful and superior to what we're seeing in situations or in the people around us. When this happens, it is easy to play into self-denial about our personal shortcomings, and it blinds us from our own character flaws.

When this happens, it shows that our judgments and ego are more a reflection of our wounded heart and personality. Realizing this about ourselves and finding techniques to overcome these issues, with honesty reflection, is a big step to healing past wounds.

Here are a few techniques to practice and help heal the judgment and ego wounds we have. Intentionally working on these steps will transform you and your relationships, strengthen your communication skills and build confidence within yourself.

- **Learn to have more empathy. Empathy is the ability to emotionally understand what other people feel, see things from their perspective, and imagine yourself in their place.**
- **Notice when your thoughts become negative, even if they are about yourself. Resolve to change those thoughts into positive thoughts will impact how you see the world around you. Doing this with others helps expand your empathy skills.**
- **Learn to reframe your thoughts. This fits perfectly with changing negative talk into positive talk. Finding an alternative way to consider your self-talk plays in to a more open-hearted approach to understanding people. An example is being cut off in traffic by another person. It may make you angry, but consider the other driver may be having a medical emergency and is trying to get help. If we realize what the other person is going through, it changes your perspective about a situation.**
- **Stop making everything that happens about you. Most**

things that happen in our daily life are not a personal attack or meant to harm us. These frustrating instances are probably caused by a previous incident that you may or may not have been involved in.

· Learn the difference between REACTING and RESPONDING. These words seem similar, but actually learning to apply this tactic will change how you control your emotions. In the article "A Simple Formula For Responding Not Reacting", we read that reacting is quick. Responding is slower. Responding creates more space between an event and what you do (or don't do) with it. In that space, you give immediate emotions some room to breathe, better understand what is happening, make a plan using the most evolved part of your brain, then go forward accordingly.

· Be curious about people without a motive for asking questions. Most people are delighted to talk about themselves. Having a curious nature builds trust with people. It also makes them feel valued and included. Understanding why people do the things they do is the cornerstone to strong connections.

· Work on positive personal development. Learning about personalities, confidence building, leadership skills and living intentionally are just a few topics that improve our self-esteem but also make us see the big picture in life. We are a cog in the wheel of many lives. If we get out of control or inflated, we don't fit well into the process and our wheel isn't helpful.

When you judge others, you tend to judge yourself more. Take the time to stop judging yourself. It will free your heart and mind.

"Think from the heart, not the ego" -unknown

"Before you assume, learn the facts. Before you judge, understand why. Before you hurt someone, feel. Before you speak, think." — Helen Barry

6

Chapter 6

The Alliance of Validation and Empathy

"**E**mpathy is seeing with the eyes of another, listening with the ears of another and feeling with the heart of another." — **Alfred Adler**

"The validation of the thoughts and emotions of others is more important than the want to be heard." — **unknown**

Having empathy is one of the biggest tools to have in your communication resource toolbox. Without the ability to use empathy, you will find that people will not connect to you, trust you or want to be influenced by you.

What is Empathy?

A mental connection with another person due to their experience of emotions, thoughts, or attitudes.

What is Validation?

The act of affirming a person, or their ideas, feelings, actions, etc., as acceptable and worthy

Empathy and validation are so closely tied that it is difficult to have one without the other.

Both empathy and validation, however, need to have clear personal boundaries.

Feeling or having empathy toward another person or experience does not mean you have to assume the problems or circumstances of that person. Using empathy calls for awareness of what's going on, not responsibility for what's going on or what has happened. Empathy is not the same as feeling sympathy for a person or situation. Sympathy is feeling sadness, pity or heartache about something or someone. Empathy is neither sad or happy, or even an emotion. It is a form of understanding that the other person has a state of mind behind a given situation.

Validation or validating another person's thoughts, feelings or decisions, similarly, does not imply that you agree with them. You don't even need to have an opinion. Essentially, validation allows you, as the listener, to move forward with a conversation without an assessment of what happened. It allows you to just gather information, make the other person feel at ease, while breaking down any barriers that existed.

Knowing the limits and boundaries of empathy and validation can help us foster strong conversations by being confident of what we allow ourselves to believe. A healthy approach to communication can enhance trust and ultimately lead to improved relationships.

Simply put, you establish that you understand what they are feeling without trying to talk them out of it or shame them for their feelings.

Showing validation can be as simple as sitting comfortably and relaxed, remaining peaceful and interested. Ask questions to show how much you are listening, or to convey you'd like to better understand what they are telling you. Always avoid commenting about blame in the other person's situation. It is important to make the speaker feel valued, affirming that you care about and accept the person as they are.

Validating statements are statements or expressions used in communication to acknowledge and affirm someone's feelings, thoughts, or experiences. Here are a few great examples:

- **"I understand how you feel."**
- **"It's okay to feel that way."**
- **"I hear what you're saying."**
- **"I can see why you would think that."**
- **"You have every right to be upset."**
- **"That must be really hard for you."**
- **"I appreciate you sharing this with me."**
- **"Your feelings are valid."**
- **"I'm here for you."**

· "I'm sorry that you're going through this."

"I've learned that people will forget what you said, people will forget what you did, but people will never forget how you made them feel." — Maya Angelou

7

Chapter 7

Embracing with an Open Mind and Heart

Living with an open heart is all about holding space for ourselves, so we can respect who we are, heal and find even more space in our bodies where we can open up even deeper. — **Melissa Trentadue**

"Open your heart, and you will find that kindness and compassion come naturally to you." — unknown

The act of being *open-minded* involves being opener receptive to different concepts, statements, and information. It doesn't mean you have to agree or believe the thoughts being stated. It just means you are willing to hear them.

Being *open-hearted* meaning that you are choosing to look through the eye of love, joy, and compassion at people and the world around you.

Living open-hearted can be difficult, especially if you are sensitive. It is important not to take on the problems or the stress of another person you are being open-hearted to. To maintain composure, and your own sense of self, it's imperative to have boundaries.

A simple smile, a kind word or even offering a bottle of water are small examples of living open-hearted. We don't have to solve people's problems, but we can be encouraging and uplifting to them. Your kindness might make the difference between life and death for someone one day.

Listening to people with an open mind and an open heart can break down emotional barriers, bringing healing to relationships.

Doctor Yvette Erasmus states on her site that as our strong heart emerges, we will find the following:

- **We stop controlling and possessing other people, and we stop allowing ourselves to be controlled or possessed.**
- **We see our relationship as crucibles that mirror and reflect aspects of ourselves – both light and dark – so that we can learn to love up all the parts.**
- **We find ways of being in committed relationships while still being free.**
- **We stop imposing ourselves and our values on others, and we stop sacrificing ourselves or living into values that are not authentically ours.**

- We learn how to express our anger while remaining loving toward one another.
- We see our faults and our growth edges while maintaining our sense of dignity and worth.
- We can be both deeply connected to each other while protecting our boundaries and ourselves.
- We find ways of being deeply self-nurturing while remaining generous towards others.

Everything changes when we learn to listen for what might be in someone's heart instead of focusing on how or what they said.

It's easier to remain calm, allowing us to respond and not quickly react. This helps us grow, learn, trust, and empower ourselves and those we interact with. Try it, it works like magic!

"Listening is a magnetic and strange thing, a creative force. The friends who listen to us are the ones we move toward. When we are listened to, it creates us, makes us unfold and expand." — Karl A. Menniger

"To say that a person feels listened to means a lot more than just their ideas get heard. It's a sign of respect. It makes people feel valued." — Deborah Tannen

8

Chapter 8

Become the Ultimate Listener and The Person
Everyone Loves to Talk To

"Most of the successful people I've known are the ones who do more listening than talking."—Bernard Baruch

If you've made it this far, you have found numerous reasons why it's important to be a great conversationalist. I believe it is a personal life skill worth studying and implementing. So far, we have covered many techniques to try to help you become a more productive communicator.

One of the first books I read on my personal development journey was "How to Win Friends and Influence People" by Dale Carnegie. It gave some essential techniques I still use today.

Some key points made by Dale Carnegie are:

- **Develop a genuine interest in others. You'll be more of an influence on people with fast results by becoming interested in other people. Do this by listening intently and asking questions.**
- **Don't be critical of the person. Criticism hurts a person's sense of importance, hurts his precious pride, and arouses resentment. When we criticize, we don't make lasting changes and people often feel angry. Challenge the task, not the person.**
- **Give suggestions instead of giving orders. People are more likely to comply with a directive if they were involved in the planning of the project. Asking questions and welcoming input on ideas is a better method, helping people feel like they are in control.**

"How to Win Friends and Influence People", published in 1936, is the "tried and true" cornerstone to becoming an expert conversationalist. Dale Carnegie's tips include:

- **Be a good listener. Encourage others to talk about themselves.**
- **Make the other person feel important — and do it sincerely.**
- **Let the other person do a great deal of the talking.**
- **Try honestly to see things from the other person's standpoint.**
- **Let the other person feel that the idea is his or hers.**
- **Use their first name in conversation. People respond well when you call them by name, it is personal and pleasing to**

their ears.

In today's society, what Dale Carnegie was pointing to and instructing us to do is what we call Emphatic Active Listening. It's all about making a good and lasting connection. Study the process, implement the process, and then teach the process.

People will want to know your secret!

9

Chapter 9

Conclusion

Today's influencers and business leaders can connect with their team members and respond to them positively by offering encouragement, help, and safety when they're down.

Being a successful leader isn't easy. They need that special "something" to maintain that success. When you take the time to invest in people, you will always win. Earn their trust, earn their loyalty, earn their respect. Be believable! Be trustworthy! Be authentic!

An open ear is the only believable sign of an open heart. — David W Augsburger

"Be a light not a judge. Be a model not a choice. be part of the solution not part of the problem." — Stephen Covey

**If you found the book helpful, please leave me an Amazon Review. Thank you!

www.ingramcontent.com/pod-product-compliance
Lightning Source LLC
Chambersburg PA
CBHW070749260726

48660CB00007B/3041